BLESSINGS ABOUND

A devotional book of channelled prayers

Written by Grigoria Kritsotelis

Copyright © 2023 Grigoria Kritsotelis

All rights reserved. No part of this book may be reproduced, distributed or used in any other manner without written permission of the copyright owner, except for the use of quotations in a book review or certain non-commercial uses permitted by copyright law. For more information or permission requests, write to the publisher, address grigoriakritsotelis@gmail.com

ISBN: 978-0-6451609-2-5

Independently Published

FIRST EDITION

Front Cover Image Design by Stacey Jessop

Transcribed by Olivia Anderson

Edited by Rachel White

First printed edition 2023

www.grigoriakritsotelis.com

DEDICATION

To God, it's all you.

CONTENTS

Preface	9
Volume One	11
Volume Two	235
Final Words	233
About the Author	235

PREFACE

These aren't just a collection of prayers. Each prayer has been channelled and has encoded within it the light of God. Each carries codes beyond what words will ever be able to contain or express. Each will take you on a personal journey if you allow it to. Use them as you desire, but also use them as part of your spiritual practice. Prayer is powerful.

During their birth, each one would tell me the ideal time to be used, and I debated sharing that with you. But then God offered me a reflection; they told me when it was best for me to use each of them, and they will tell you the same. And it is likely that they will offer each of us something different in a moment that is unique to us all.

As much as these moved through me as expressions of God, they came through you too, as you prayed for answers, the words that would offer you the medicine you needed was birthed in that moment. And here is your medicine.

I implore you to use the empty pages between prayers to create your own. You can also take my prayers and add parts that you need or remove others. This book is designed to be a healing tool, a connection tool and a divination tool. It is your magic just as much as it is mine.

The way in which you use this prayer book is up to you, my recommendation is for you to read it cover to cover the first time around, and then from then on, to use it the same way you would use an Oracle Deck, and open up to a random page each day or night and it will offer you what you need.

At the end of the book, I have offered you all a space where you can submit your own prayers to create more volumes, so that the world can know your light too.

Life is a constant dance with the Divine. Let your relationship with God be your most important, every other relationship will follow that one. Regularly communicate with the Divine, so much so that conversing with God seems like second nature.

BLESSINGS ABOUND

VOLUME ONE

Use the blank pages as a prayer canvas for you to channel your own Divine Prayers, if and when you're called to. God moves through each of us - listen to the whispers, they are songs and activations that will offer you the medicine you need.

BLESSINGS ABOUND

1

Divine Guidance, I call upon my infinite self into this moment, may I feel the totality of who I am take space in this moment. Allow this sacred journey to be protected and amplified by light. Allow me to recognise myself as a channel, an ever-flowing channel, always connected, and allow the messages to come through me in such a way that I can easily understand and interpret them. Allow it to always be easy and effortless because I know that it can be. Let me recognise that the infinite supply isn't just what I'm a part of, but what flows through me at all times - and I can allow as much or as little of the infinite supply to move through me as I desire. Let me see all limitations as the illusions that they really are and remind me that I am in fact God in flesh experiencing the 3D world because my soul was honoured to experience expansion in this way. I thank you for bringing this soul family into my experience at the perfect time. I foresee the collective shifts that will be birthed by our collective prayer and work together. Thank you. I love you. And so it is. Amen.

2

Divine Guidance, today I call upon my own surrender. I acknowledge that true surrender is accepting things as they are without the desire or need to change them, including all feelings that reside in my physical body. I acknowledge that all things are divine and that each play a Divine role, one that I accept lovingly. I recognise that all feelings and perceptions, I have allowed willingly, and that transcendence is always an option, but it must be preceded with acceptance and non-judgement. That is true connection with source. I ask that you show me more ways to offer acceptance, non-judgement, and surrender. I recognise that the call for growth will also call for contrast, but with you guiding me, I know that it is just God discovering more of Himself. And I need not fear anything, because all is known by the infinite self, I welcome your love. I acknowledge that enlightenment is the realisation that all is well. All is as it should be. There is no disharmony, no imperfections. All is one, as it has always been. I call you to amplify the love that lies within me. And may that love be mirrored in everyone that crosses my path. May I find comfort in the contrast and may I transmute it effortlessly. Thank you. I love you. And so it is. Amen.

BLESSINGS ABOUND

3

Divine Guidance, remind us that no path is ever hidden and that all truths are truth, while acknowledging that all truths are fragments of the absolute truth. I hold onto nothing and allow everything to move through me freely with no restriction. I surrender and trust that only that which is for my highest good will pass through my experience. I trust that my all-knowing infinite self is directing this journey therefore nothing is unknown by me. The moment I call for the revelation is the moment it's received by my conscious self - like accessing a vivid memory. I am honoured to be here. And so it is. I love you. Amen.

BLESSINGS ABOUND

4

Divine Guidance, we acknowledge that we've been alchemists for eternity, never separate from our potent power. We always have the power to shift and transform energy in the 3D world. You offered us thought as the catalyst that would lead to a vibrational shift and we call upon you to forever remind us that it's the thought that leads to the behaviours, that leads to the emotion, that leads to the vibrational offering. We recognise that through our intentional offerings, we project those offerings, not just as I, but as all of me, the infinite I, my ancestors, my spirit team, my galactic ancestors, my protectors - every part of me connected to the infinite - who understands my expansive purpose here, offering me complete creative power. And when I harness that creative expression, I express with the potency of all my mastered lifetimes. Thank you for this reminder. I love you. And so it is. Amen.

BLESSINGS ABOUND

5

Divine Guidance, I call upon the amplification of my innate power. I recognise that my power is ever present - but may this declaration allow me to realise the magnitude of that power. Anything conceivable is real - there are no exceptions. May this journey unravel all things that are to be known by my conscious self in this lifetime. May I recognise that calling upon you to move through me is all that will ever be required of me. I am as I believe I am, and I believe that you are me - the limitless infinite expression incarnated into this magnificent vessel that moves through the fabric of life as if it were an intimate dance with the all mighty. Oh, how blessed I am. I love you. And so it is. Amen.

6

Divine Guidance, I call upon my natural gifts. I acknowledge that I perceive them as spiritual gifts, but I remember that they have been with me since my genesis. I ask that you help me release anything that is resisting my connection to Source. The art of Divination, as perceived by humans is the seeking of knowledge of the unknown by supernatural means - but we recognise that we need not seek, instead just allow the natural flow, the natural currents to move gracefully through us, as nothing is unknown by the infinite self. It is just being remembered and interpreted by the conscious self. And the supernatural is merely the supernatural after the illusions of separation have been lifted. Tapping into my natural state is easy - and only requires my devotion and attention. And so it is. Amen.

BLESSINGS ABOUND

7

Divine Guidance, I call upon you for Godly amplification. I immerse myself and become one with your Golden Light - and I feel my entire body of frequency shift into one in alignment with the healing Golden Light. And as I become it, so too, I radiate it, anything I touch, think about or am in close proximity to becomes this Golden healing Light, a protection shield that deflects anything that isn't of light and absorbs all that is of light. Remind me that my intention and will create my holographic perceived reality. And so, I choose to be in alignment with the highest graces and highest frequencies. I call upon my light being ancestors to be present in everything I do, think, and say. Allow my magic's potency to carry the codes of my ancestors, my angels, and my Spiritual Team. I am of light. I embody light, I am light. I am. And so it is. I love you. Thank you. Amen.

BLESSINGS ABOUND

8

Divine Guidance, I feel the veil lift, I feel myself shift into new depths. It's almost impossible to explain, but I feel myself being simultaneously the microcosm of the microcosm and the macrocosm of the macrocosm. As minute to realise that nothing matters, and as magnificent to know that it all does. It feels like a loop - I'm within everything so deeply that it creates an entire new expansive Universe. Today I recognise, offering no resistance at all, that there is no power outside of me - all powers exist within me and require only my will to activate them and master them. There are infinite electrical charges moving through my physical vessel and my energetic body and auric field. And I know that my mind alone can alter the frequencies that move through me. Today I consciously and intentionally activate my ability to manipulate those charges and direct them to connect with anything I desire. If I am everything, then everything is me. The cloud, the flame, the stone, the water is no less me than the hands, the feet and the mouth that I recognise as me. I ask you to support and amplify this activation. Thank you. I love you. And so it is. Amen.

BLESSINGS ABOUND

9

Divine Guidance, today I call upon your protection as I move through the illusions of linear time and space. As I continue to tap into your energy and infinite wisdom, I realise more and more just how grande the fabric of time, as we on Earth imagine it to be is, in comparison to how it is when perceived from the All Knowing. From your omnipresence, I recognise that all is. It's all happening now, the past, present, future, exists as a circle of layers. Just as easily as I can tap into past timelines, I can tap into future ones. I know that my conscious mind will try to reject this belief and experience at times, so I choose to observe this from an all-seeing, all-knowing perspective, one where limitations don't exist and my ability to tap into any reality across any plane of existence, any density and any dimensions, is absolute. The veil is lifted, and I asked to perceive this as you would have me perceive this - beyond my conscious understanding and into the Quantum Reality. I am honoured to experience life in this way. Thank you, I love you. And so it is. Amen.

BLESSINGS ABOUND

10

Divine Guidance, every day I come to you, and you bestow upon me the codes, wisdom and guidance required to navigate this experience. I take none of it for granted, and recognise that I have actively and intentionally stretched beyond my perceived confinements of reality, and you continue revealing to me the doorways and pathways that lead to more. Never could have I imagined expansiveness in this way - yet I simultaneously acknowledge that even as I experience expansion, it is limited by my human condition, and yet you show me more. Today I ask that any illusions of confinement, that still exist in my consciousness, slip away, so that what is left is truth - a truth that I need not understand, but a truth that allows me to stretch to every crevice of reality, as you know it, not as I imagine it to be. I allow myself to be an open channel for this wisdom and I ask that you protect me with White and Golden Light. I surrender and allow you to navigate. I am ready for the next unlocking. And so it is. I love you. Amen.

11

Divine Guidance, I, as the light, honour the parts of me that dwell in the shadows. I offer no judgement and recognise that they are just as Divinely created as embodiments and expressions of you. Beyond my body and mind, I can witness the shadows that exist in this plane of existence, and here too, I recognise their Divine Orchestration. All is allowed to exist and it is all serving. We either honour the light that we are and amplify that light or resist and reject that light. Both are serving. Polarity and duality reminds me that Source, although a light/love frequency - is all-encompassing and neutral. All expressions of self were to be experienced - even those we perceive as dark/dense. And it remains that God lives within those expressions too. I accept that I am of the light and always protected by that light even when I explore the shadow aspects of Source. The shadows exist merely because we run into debris and distractions on this plane which distort our true essence. I am safe and I am light. And so it is. I love you. Amen.

BLESSINGS ABOUND

12

Divine Guidance, remind me that it's infinite and eternal - that accessing all of you will forever and always be available to me. And just as easily as I can inhale the air that abounds, I can inhale infinite awareness. Your essence is held within every atom, and I need not try - merely allow what is. I acknowledge my exponential expansion and allow the codes to activate within me as they need to throughout this lifetime and all the lifetimes that preceded this one, and all that will follow. As I continue to tap into your Divine Wisdom, I recognise my role in offering wisdom to every past version of me, and offering Mastery to every future version of me. It's all here and now, nothing is denied, and all is allowed. My quest is not to understand, judge, nor identify, it is merely to submerge myself into all experiences, remembering that I am simultaneously in it, observing it and choosing it. Whenever wisdom is required, it will be offered - I need not seek more than is required in this moment, because in the doing so, I attach myself to expectations and outcomes. All is known by the infinite self, and as I continue to maintain my natural state of alignment, I continue to be directed by the

BLESSINGS ABOUND

infinite itself. Thank you for the opportunity to understand you in this way. And so it is. I love you. Amen.

BLESSINGS ABOUND

13

Divine Guidance, I call upon your light for immediate protection and healing. I call upon the love and energy of all my ancestors in all my timelines. I call for the Universe to protect me, for my guides to protect me, for Earth, the Mother, to protect me, for my Higher Self to protect me. I am Divinely protected. And as I am all, unified in Divine Light, we are all protected. There are no others. I declare that right now I release any and all energies, thoughts, and intentions that no longer serve the highest good - be them mine or another. I solidify timelines that align with my Highest Good, and the Highest Good of this planet. I cleanse myself, this space and humanity of negativity or anything not of love, across all planes of existence, universes, and timelines. Let your Divine Light and protection bathe me. Guide me to move through any perceived pain, recognising that the shadows are of God too, and only require illumination. Allow me to feel the love that I am. Transmute any judgement I may have to perceived darkness, allow me to see the Divinity in all things, people, and experiences, there are no mistakes, only Divine Orchestration. I call upon the Universe to transmute the heaviness and density we are all carrying

as a collective, make it easy for us to release it. Allow us to tap into our bodies for the Divine Wisdom it offers us. Soften our walls so that we feel safe fully surrendering to your Divine Light, knowing that nothing but light/love can exist in our field unless we allow it to. Remind us that we can observe the shadows but not absorb them. Remind us that we are never denied your Divine Grace. Remind us that infinite love is always flowing through us and from us, and that we can access it at any time we wish. Remind us that our will is powerful, and with conviction and attention can solidify timelines, and we choose Light - United in Love. May the whole world, and all those past, present, and future, feel the love that has been planted here today through this prayer, and may we know ourselves as God knows us - a perfect embodiment of the Divine. May we feel this shift towards light immediately. We call for your immediate intervention. In gratitude, love, wellness, light, and peace. Only love may exist here. I pray for all my brothers and sisters, may they feel their field shift, may they know the depth of God's infinite love. And so it is. I love you. Thank you. Amen.

14

Divine Guidance, I call upon you to amplify my Divinity. Show me how powerful I am. I recognise that I was born magnetic - drawing all that I am unto me – and I call upon you to amplify my magnetism. Allow me to release any resistance or blocks that are creating a veil between my current experienced reality and my highest timeline. I release any resistance lovingly, and as I feel the density soften and dissolve, I simultaneously welcome the illuminated pathways. I recognise that I am choosing to align with my highest timeline, and the only thing required of me is my devotion. I am devoted to embodying my highest timeline. I ask for your immediate intervention to help me move through anything I may not yet see as a distraction or distortion, and offer me the faith, strength, and courage to move forward with clarity, conviction, and confidence. I feel these shifts immediately. Thank you. I love you. And so it is. Amen.

BLESSINGS ABOUND

15

*Divine Guidance, illuminate my magic. I know that I am an individualised expression of you with unique coding that only I contain - therefore my desire to express myself is you experiencing yourself through me - wanting expansion. I will no longer deny my desire to be more of everything. Make it easy for me to hear your whispers navigating the path, remind me to let go and let you take the wheel - as it's **you** experiencing yourself through me - you are the driver - and I surrender to my higher calling. Remind me that my magic has been Divinely planted, and there are those who pray for revelations that are being answered through me. May everything that I am be amplified by you as I consciously choose to connect to your infinity. No part of me is small, I embody the grandest seas, skies, galaxies, and beyond. I choose to remember how much flows through me when I allow it to. I ask that you always offer me soft whispers to remind me of my grandness. Thank you. I love you. And so it is. Amen.*

16

Divine Guidance, I call upon you to amplify everything that I am - my true self. Remind me that I transcend time and space - and the thought alone brings it into my field of awareness, because time is not linear, so the physical realisation preceded the thought - but it was planted into my awareness by my future self. Help me simplify your Divine Wisdom in such a way that it becomes effortless to integrate. Use me to express yourself the way you intended to be expressed; Divine, love-filled, expansive, and whole. Let me see all possibilities as probabilities if they feel like truth in my body. Remind me to work from higher Consciousness, the Quantum Field, to observe as you observe - as already done and destined if I choose it and will it into being. Allow me to surrender and trust the unravelling - keeping focused but with a loose grip - allowing space for you to surprise me, bewilder me, redirect me to my highest path. My faith in the Divine Orchestration is unwavering. The thoughts - divinely guided, the redirections, divinely guided. And so it is. I love you. Amen.

17

Divine Guidance, I ask for clarity. Make it easy for me to discern what is truth and what is my resistance to truth. Make it easy for me to flow into alignment using the tools that you've planted into my awareness. Remind me that I already have it all and I have immediate access to even what I perceive as the remotest options - as you are omnipresent, therefore I am omnipresent - and channelling your wisdom is just me channelling the part of me who is all-knowing and offers no resistance. Whenever I find myself drifting away from myself - bring these tools back into my awareness to remind me that flowing is effortless, but not without effort. I trust the messages. And so it is. I love you. Amen.

BLESSINGS ABOUND

18

Divine Guidance, thank you for reminding me that you're in everything. I know sometimes I live my life detached from the reality of your omnipresence - but you constantly offer me your soft whispers - and they never go unnoticed. I know it's not my job to know the complexities of the human experience and how interconnected it is with every part of the Universe - even the parts my mind cannot conceive, and still you offer me a roadmap - allowing me to simplify the inconceivable. You offer me light codes, energy centres, crystalline structures, multiple bodies, thought, imagination, everything I could possibly need to understand you. I commit to devote myself to understanding you more - and as I understand you, I understand me. And I will not look out there for answers - I will look within - because herein is where the answers lie. I open myself up to the steady and consistent flow of the Universal ether - moving through me like a poetic current of Divinity. I am honoured to be here, experiencing you in this way. And so it is. I love you. Amen.

BLESSINGS ABOUND

19

Divine Guidance, today I call for your Godly amplification. I cannot possibly conceive my grandness, and yet you show me. Make the signs even more telling, make it easy for me to remember that my will is thy will. Remind me just how playful all of this gets to be. The Divine Web is perfectly orchestrated. I need not resist it, instead I accept it, flow with it, embrace it, and play with it. You offered me a blueprint to understand myself better - may I forever realise that the cosmic web is at my service. I need only call upon you to illuminate. I recognise that although the earthly experience has a long wait list, so the honour to be here and experience all of this is profound, the veil of forgetting plants seeds of separateness. Remind me that not even the dust particle that resides on even the remotest planet is separate from me - and as I will for it, I call upon it and its resonance. I feel my absoluteness and I embrace the byproduct of that absoluteness. I speak of my grandness with conviction and with love. I love you. Thank you. And so it is. Amen.

20

Divine Guidance, may I forever find bliss in the unravelling. Remind me to be curious and playful here. It's not so serious. It was always supposed to feel sensorially real, so much so that I get caught up in the illusion of it - forgetting that I'm the one in control. But I remember now - remember that I am the surfer choosing the best waves and I need not keep falling under water fighting the currents, trying to find my way back. But instead, I embrace a continuous riding of the infinite waves, choosing as I desire which feel the most exciting. Let me incarnate again and again until I have fully embraced the joy and expansion that I get to experience here. May I recognise the cosmic loop that is designed to always offer me reminders that what I desire lives within me first, as above, so below, as within, so without. The details don't matter so much - but the unravelling, the choosing, the bliss - that is what I signed up for. I choose to lead with this awareness, and I vow never to forget that I am the observer, the observed, and the creator all at once. I love you. Thank you. And so it is. Amen.

21

Divine Guidance, there's no place grander than right here and right now - so may I always remember to be all in, basking in the glory of the present moment, for it is where you'd have me be for eternity. My every wish is your wish, and may I act in accordance with that knowing. May I be reminded to love myself as you love me – unconditionally, and may the overflow of love pour onto those around me, and may it be felt by everyone and everything, past, present, future, the omnipresent now. I vow to stay committed to my faith, I will show up fully immersed in this life. May I find pleasure in all of it, may you remind me of your humour, and may I lead with the curiosity of a human, while honouring the whispers of the infinite who does not need to be curious. May I forever see myself in others, as there are no others, may my triggers dissipate and may my magic be potent and amplify as I continue to remember and master my power. Use me as you desire, may it always be for the highest good for me and others. Tell me what you would have me do, and I will honour the call. Thank you. I love you. And so it is. Amen.

22

Divine Guidance, I am open to receive you fully, I asked you to use me, work through me, show me my Divine purpose. Reveal to me the tools and shortcuts, show me how powerful I am. I will do my part to activate those codes, to strengthen them, to amplify them and most of all, to use them. Show me that the veil is an illusion, that unity is the only true form, and that includes unity between worlds and dimensions. Make it easy for me to realise that I can step in and out of any timeline at will - remind me to consciously choose the path that is for my highest good - while listening to your direction. Receive this prayer as my offering to activate the codes of amplification, healing, and the removal of the veil. I take these keys with great responsibility, I feel them change the frequency in my body immediately. These light codes are now activated, and I will use them at will. May I enter this new journey as this new version of me. I enter the open portal now. I am safe and protected on this journey. Thank you. And so it is. I love you. Amen.

23

Divine Guidance, awaken me. Allow me to see more than I have previously been able to perceive. Let me see through your eyes. Beyond the earthly realm, I am a multi-dimensional force of infinite wisdom, power, and love. May I feel this activation, may it feel like something awakens within me and I am forever changed. I call upon the Highest Beings of Light to aid me on my journey. I call upon all the Archangels and my Spirit Team to guide me to my Highest Timeline. I grant them permission to intervene if it's for my highest good or my protection. Align me with the people, places, and communities that will amplify my ability to connect with your Divine Word. May my words be your words, may my will be your will. I call upon my immediate ability to realise my Divine Oneness with all things, and as I will for my energy field to shift and morph, I can will for the energy field of anything to shift and morph. Forever remind me that I am light embodied, here to serve and remind humanity of our Oneness. And so it is. I love you. Thank you. Amen.

24

Divine Guidance, I am ready to remember more than my limited perception that has been contained here in this 3D world - I acknowledge that I have ancestors in many Galaxies, on many planets, whom all share with me their wisdom and light codes - forever waiting for me to accept them fully so that they will be activated within me. They offer me messages and guidance, allow me to translate and interpret these messages in the most effortless way. Nothing is unknown by the infinite me - so I call upon the wisdom that is of service now, I accept it lovingly, knowing that it leads to my highest good. My ability to tap into this level of Divine Wisdom shows me that my mission here is beyond what I've previously imagined it to be. I open myself up to more, while asking you to support my capacity to receive, allow my body to ascend so that I can contain more light codes - that my dense body has previously rejected. I am ready. Thank you. I love you. And so it is. Amen.

25

Divine Guidance, thank you. You have never denied me access to infinity - but now I remember how to intentionally tap into that infinity and choose what and how I experience this plane of reality. You offer me tools and codes to amplify the potency of what I choose to tap into. Protect me with Divine Light as I allow infinity to move through me. May any perceived limitations dissipate and may I realise that the illusion of confinement I perceive as a human in a physical body is just that - an illusion. My infinity cannot be contained, it can only ever be temporarily explored in the now. I choose to always act from a place of knowing that my infinite self is accessible to me at all times and only requires my choosing. I trust that you will always guide me to choose the expression and experience that is for my Highest Good. I surrender to the unfolding knowing that it is the natural byproduct of choosing to experience the enfolded. I feel expansive as I proclaim this to you. Thank you. I love you. And so it is. Amen.

BLESSINGS ABOUND

26

Divine Guidance. I recognise that the perceivable Universe is beyond my current comprehension - but I ask that you expand the scope in which I can receive the awareness of your grandness. I trust that I am here now, open to this level of awareness, because you have invited me to be here now. This present moment is the key that unlocks the codes to Infinite Awareness. I have been preparing for this for lifetimes. What is to be revealed to me will serve the collective expansion and I trust that I will know what to do with all that you unlock within me. It is a great honour to do this work in this lifetime and I vow to remember this work in every lifetime. As I activate it now, it lives with me for eternity - as it has always. It is impossible to be separate from the truth. And that truth is love, unity with the Infinite Creator and the infinite expressions of the Infinite Creator. I recognise my responsibility to be of service and I lead with that intention. May you guide the way, illuminating the people, places, and catalysts required on my journey. Thank you. I love you. And so it is. Amen.

BLESSINGS ABOUND

27

Divine Guidance, guide me in making the unconscious conscious. Relax my nervous system so that I offer no distortions to truth. Amplify my senses so that they feel so loud, yet soft, that it is impossible to overlook the whispers. I trust my ability to access the unseen, because you exist through me. Lead me into mastery, I offer my will and intention and create the space, time, and attention to master all gifts that you have activated within me. I do this alongside my Spiritual Team, my ancestors who offer wisdom, coding, and protection, my angels who offer guidance, messages, and protection, my Spirit Guides who align me with my Highest Timeline, whom I grant permission to intervene if that timeline is threatened, and my Galactic Family who offer me codes, activations, and initiations. As I weave the web, you weave it through me. As I create and expand, so too do I understand, perceive, and expand some more. There is no need, there is only space to create, express, and expand. It's all allowed, and I choose for it to be my Highest Timeline, for the greatest good of all involved. I am honoured to do this work. Thank you. I love you. And so it is. Amen.

BLESSINGS ABOUND

28

Divine Guidance, we invite ourselves into the open portal, knowing that as we step in, we will see as you see, beyond limits and confinements. We welcome all messages that are serving, as though we have chosen them to be revealed. We do not seek from a place of curiosity, we merely become consciously aware of natural resonance. Use me as a Divine Channel. May I be a channel of Divine Light/Love. And may I use those messages to be of service to the highest order. I trust the wisdom I receive, acknowledging you in them. Enlighten me so that I know how to use the messages, codes, and activations. Support my desires so that I can work at my fullest capacity, as my desires are just your desires for me. May ease flow through my life, making my Spiritual Practice effortless. Teach me how to replenish post Spiritual Practice at Quantum Speed. I call upon you for immediate intervention. I feel every cell in my body dancing with the Divine, may my blessings abound, may my prayers create ripples, and may I eternally remember my Divine Light. Thank you. I love you. And so it is. Amen.

BLESSINGS ABOUND

29

Divine Guidance, remind me that nothing more is required. That all is. And when I focus on the here and now and detach from the details, I offer no resistance at all. Nothing needs to be acquired - I am given the cues when I should access codes, information, or frequency directly from you, and I need not carry them as heavy trophies, I use them and with love and then once that code has been activated and opened, I release it lovingly. I exist in the one shared awareness, may I act accordingly. I have opened the portal, no doorway being closed or unavailable to me, and so I need not rush. I let it all flow with ease, and I offer the necessary space, time, and reverence required for the sacred exchange. May I forever see you and everything. I am one with the perfect Divine Order. And so it is. Thank you. I love you. Amen.

BLESSINGS ABOUND

30

Divine Guidance, work through me. Use me as a portal for your Divine Light. I call upon my angels, ancestors, and Spirit Guides to offer light and protection. I pray that I am surrounded by your infinite love. I am a channel for your Divine Grace. Please allow all messages to be revealed in a way that I can understand and interpret them. I call for only love to exist within my sacred channel and for me to be protected. I ask that I effortlessly access the light codes and activations required for the next part of my journey. I ask that the messages are loud and clear. I ask that the portal closes when the channel is complete. May I see as you see, may I offer this light to others to be of service for the highest good of all involved. I ask that these transmissions offer blessings to all involved. I trust that the messages revealed will be easily and effortlessly integrated by everyone involved. May the revelation alone begin the transmutation process. May there be a softening as you grace it with your Light and Divine Love. Thank you. I love you. And so it is. Amen.

BLESSINGS ABOUND

31

The glory of you God - I feel it tremendously. Your love - the infinity of it - I can feel it completely. I'll never truly be able to embody it fully because I'll never be able to truly understand it - but I know it's there - in every crevice that has ever existed - it is there - it is. Exponential transcendence, that's what I'm experiencing - everything is flowing into place, and I am grateful; grateful in a way that words could never truly harness my gratitude - but now I want more. I am allowing more of myself to be realised. I am ready to let it in. Show me. Show me what abundance, freedom, opportunities, love, truly is. Show me more of myself - I'm ready to feel more of me. Show me the way to myself - to you. Allow me to tap into my channelling abilities - reveal my gifts so that I can serve in the way that I desire. LOVE is the way, and it is the only way I choose. If it is of love - reveal it to me. Guide me, I have faith that you are always with me, directing me, but now, I'm ready for more. I am crystal clear with my intentions - light the path - so that I can see myself. I love you. From the part of me that IS YOU. I love you. And so it is. Amen.

BLESSINGS ABOUND

32

Divine Guidance, I call upon the angels, ancestors of light, spirit guides, and spiritual team. I ask that you be present here as we bless the soul of _____ (insert name) as she/he transitions from this world to the next. I pray that she/he feels the love that she/he is. We recognise that as we refer to her/him, as she/he in this ceremony, that she/he is now one with her/his infinite self and far beyond the confined perception of she/he that existed in the 3D world. But as we refer to her/him as she/he, we allow ourselves to tap into her/his earthly resonance. We pray that strength and enlightenment engulf her/him. We pray that she/he remembers the infinity of souls, and that the temporary physical journey she/he has come from was designed to teach her/him love, and when the soul is ready, it will always choose to move on. We pray that she/he is showered in Golden Light, so that her/his shadows see their own light. We pray that any perceived pain that she/he carried in the 3D world is healed and transmuted so that it will not come with her/him into the next life. We pray that she/he remembers her/his own Divinity - and that remembering leads to joy, alignment, and unconditional love. We acknowledge that all of this would have been realised

the moment she/he transitioned, but as time is not linear, as we pray for her/him now, her/his transition then was made easier. May peace be upon her/him, and may she/he eternally feel the love that has been planted here through this prayer. And so it is. Amen.

BLESSINGS ABOUND

33

Divine Guidance, I call upon your immediate intervention. I call upon your Divine Light. I recognise that I am eternally connected to your light - I ask that you help me remember, I ask that I feel light the way you feel it. I acknowledge that my human body cannot always keep up with my spiritual progress and growth - so I call upon all my guides, ancestors of light, angels, and spiritual team to soften the perceived pain felt by my body - remind every cell I carry in this body that it is healed, healthy, and whole. I call upon your immediate intervention - and as I call, it is received and answered. I remind myself that my job is to believe that the call has been answered, and act accordingly. Let me see the light that you are in myself - even when I think I can't. Let me feel alignment, as you know alignment - not as I have imagined it to be. Remind me, whenever the 3D world consumes me, that I am the stars, the sun, the moon, the sky. Remind me that I was born in perfect harmony and any discord or resistance I feel is a byproduct of this world, and I have the means and power to move through the heaviness and feel my light once again. I call upon your light. Thank you. I love you. And so it is. Amen.

BLESSINGS ABOUND

34

Divine Guidance, I call upon the peace that I am - acknowledging that any and all barriers preventing me from that peace, have been built here and now, and at any moment I can choose to move past those barriers and remember that as I am of you - my Divinity is absolute. Remind me that this applies to all my perceptions in this 3D world. Anything I think I do not yet have is just the illusion of separation that I have created here and now, and that at any moment I have the power to remember that the illusion isn't real, I am real. I, as in you, I, as in everything and everyone, I, as in not just connected to all that is, but instead the literal embodiment of all that is. Remind me of this absolute truth when I perceive barriers. Remind me who I am. And so it is. I love you. Amen.

35

Divine Guidance, I call upon your infinite Grace. Allow me to hear, see, and feel the Divine Messages coming through in all people, places, and experiences. Allow me to translate the message in a way that I understand. Allow it to be easy and effortless. Let me recognise that the infinite supply isn't just what I'm a part of - but what flows through me at all times. And I can allow as much or as little of the infinite supply to move through me as I desire. Let me see all limitations as the illusions that they really are and remind me that I am in fact God in flesh - experiencing the 3D world because my soul was honoured to experience expansion in this way. I remember who I am. Thank you. I love you. And so it is. Amen.

BLESSINGS ABOUND

36

Divine Guidance, be my reference - whenever I find myself lost in this world - reveal to me who I truly am. Make the revelation soft yet clear. Allow me to realign with my natural state of being. As an infinite being experiencing this 3D world - at times I feel the pull of both worlds, individually calling for my attention. Remind me that the pull of either world, is always the pull of both - nothing is outside of infinity, therefore, all pulls are serving. I simultaneously live within infinite consciousness, and it lives within me. There may be times where I find it hard to truly understand my power, and in those moments, send me a sign - remind me that I move through this life with a Spiritual Army. What I want for me - all consciousness wants for me too - because what I, as the human self wants, I, as the collective consciousness wants too - this is expansion. Creation is the expression of frequency - what an honour to experience expansion in this way. I am as I am - and I am infinite. And so it is. I love you. Amen.

BLESSINGS ABOUND

37

Divine Guidance, I surrender to your infinite love. I feel myself become as light as a feather, and as I allow myself to fall, I feel you carry me. Sometimes it feels like a gust of wind, sometimes a small hand picks me up, and sometimes you place me on the skin of a bird so I can fly across the oceans. And as I allow myself to experience the infinite expressions of you, I remember more and more who I am. I am a poem, an art piece, a sculpture, a house, a bird, a song, a piano, an ocean, a star. And I acknowledge that all words are limited, because it is impossible to encompass our understanding of infinity in a word. Language distorts the Universal language of energy. So whenever I find myself confused, in doubt, or losing faith - remind me that the answers I seek are not found in the words, but within my own consciousness - because my consciousness is all consciousness. And in that place I am reminded of peace. Remind me that my 3D self and my infinite self are always trying to dance together in this world. The dance serves us both, because we are one and the same. So my 3D desires are wanted by all of me, and so they are never denied, all that is required is for me to allow their physical realisation,

BLESSINGS ABOUND

and the easiest way for me to do that is to feel the joy of their realisation now. Thank you for reminding me who I am. I love you. And so it is. Amen.

BLESSINGS ABOUND

38

Divine Guidance, I am honoured to be here. I acknowledge that I feel those moments of doubt, and in those moments I carry the heaviness that I have created in my mind, but you always find a way to remind me that in fact true alignment is when I choose to fully and completely surrender to the unknown. I trust that I am a clear enough channel, that I will always be able to interpret the messages and signals that are coming from my Higher Self, and I vow to always follow those nudges, because although often leading me down the path of the Unknown, that Unknown is known by my infinite self and I am safe there. I trust that everything I, as the physical self wants, all of my infinite self wants too. And I welcome it all in, as though it were a wave and I the shoreline, feeling complete and whole without it, and simultaneously knowing that together we are even more of ourselves. Let it be easy, effortless, and require only my devotional belief that God is me, and that awareness illuminates anything that may have been hidden. I step into this energy now. And so it is. Amen.

BLESSINGS ABOUND

39

Divine Guidance, I feel my light - the illumination has been received. I call upon you to witness my unbecoming. Unbecoming my conditions, limits, and seeming errors, and the remembering of my Divinity, and the Source of that which I am, which is love. And in that remembering, guide me to and through my ability to fully and completely express that love, knowing that love will always be received. And as I give it to others, remind me that I am giving it to myself. And as others give it to me, may I feel my heart expand. I am grateful for all the ways you show up for me, I know that everything is of you. Let only that which is of light enter my field, and may anything that isn't be taken by you and transmuted into light. I love you. Thank you. And so it is. Amen.

BLESSINGS ABOUND

40

Divine Guidance, I call for your support, and as I call, I realise that your support is always given to me, just the same way as my lungs allow me to breathe, it is the only way it could ever be. I am the most important energy in the Universe and so the entire Universe moves, shifts, and pivots according to my will. Make it easy for me to remember. Make it easy for me to hear your whispers that I call intuitive nudges. Allow my every decision to be made by the all-knowing part of me - the part of me detached from the confinements of this world. Allow my trust to be unwavering. Allow me to hear and interpret the messages in the most effortless way. Let it be easy. Let it be easy. Let it be easy. Let your love for me lead the way. Let me always feel the softness of love and simultaneously the full force of your love - as though it were a feather and a hurricane all at once. I am never denied, I am always connected to the infinite supply. And so it is. I love you. Amen.

BLESSINGS ABOUND

41

Divine Guidance, let me see all things as the blessings that they are; the air I breathe, the trees around me, the roof over my head, the people I meet, the random smiles, the flavours I taste, the deep belly laughs, the eyes that can cry, the trillions of cells in my body tirelessly working to keep me alive, and the photonic energy that is omnipresent that connects us all. As you allow me to effortlessly shift my perception of all things, people, and experiences, my world continues to align with my truest and highest self. Whenever I have moments where my thoughts don't align with this truth, remind me in the softest yet most clear way to come back to this truth. And from this place, all my desires are realised in physical form. I'm already connected to all things, people, and experiences, and I remember that I am God in flesh and I act accordingly. And so it is. I love you. Amen.

BLESSINGS ABOUND

42

Divine Guidance, I call upon my Spiritual Army, my ancestors, my angels, my Spirit Guides, and you - help me move through any and all perceived pain, help me feel the love that I am. Take away and transform all of the pain trapped in my physical body and my energetic body - and allow me to fully tap into my power, as a Divine Being with the ability to self-heal. Send me what I need to feel whole, worthy, safe, and loved. I call upon the energy of the entire Universe to transmute the heaviness I am carrying and to make it easy for me to release it. Soften my walls so that I feel safe letting people in to support me and hold space for me - and let me be intuitively directed to know who those people are. Remind me that infinite love is always flowing through me and that I have access to it at any time I wish. May I feel the infinite love that has been planted here through this prayer, and may I know myself as you know me - a perfect embodiment of the Divine. May I know that I am never alone. May I feel the shift towards light immediately. I call for you immediate intervention. Thank you. I love you. And so it is. Amen.

43

Divine Guidance, I call upon my truth - may what's mine be realised by me in the physical world. May anything that is resisting my alignment with it, fall away. Make it easy for me to know what's mine. If it's not for me, I ask that I don't have a want for it. If anything, or anyone is creating a barrier between me and what's mine, may they hear this call to remove themselves from my path lovingly. May I be forever guided on my path, may I feel supported on my way to what's mine. May I hear your whispers so clearly and so vividly that it feels like a conversation. May I know that I have legions upon legions of ancestors, guides, angels, and spirit supporting me, guiding me, protecting me. May they forever warn me when anything that isn't of light presents itself - but may they intervene and offer light and protection. I feel safe, loved, connected, and protected. Thank you. I love you. And so it is. Amen.

BLESSINGS ABOUND

44

Divine Guidance, today I thank you. I thank you for reminding us what love is. I acknowledge that our souls feel no pain and feel no resistance to the transition between physical and spirit. That it flows so effortlessly, like a dance between the two worlds, coming back into the physical for greater expansion, and then like a cosmic breath, returning to the Source once more. And today we witnessed the whole world shift off the strength of one human - a profound expansion of love. Every temporary human experience is an extraordinary opportunity to expand. And although hearts are aching from the perceived pain of loss and separation, it is in this moment that we are reminded of our Divinity, of our Oneness, of our Universal breath. And it's with incredible full hearts that we continue projecting that love, to those who need it, to the world, to each other. We take from one wave to give to another, and yet the ocean remains full. As I take another breath, I am reminded of what this life offers - the opportunity to expand, to experience, to create, to give… the one truth that we are - LOVE. Amen.

*Channeled when Kobe Bryant transitioned, but can be used when someone in your life transitions

45

Divine Guidance, I call upon the sacred wisdom of this land to reveal to me the powerful energetic vortex that takes my planted seeds and nurtures them so that they bear their fruits. Allow the seeds I plant in the ether, reflect intuitively back to all the actions I take. May the path be clear, may I always be guided, and may it feel easy and effortless to tune into my infinite guidance system. I am grateful for this realisation. And so it is. Amen.

46

Divine Guidance, allow me to use this amplified energy to truly see myself as the Divine Body that I am. Let me transcend beyond the conditional and limited perceptions and surrender to my own infinity. As I speak these words with conviction, I know that the part of me that offers no resistance is fully here now and is in control of the way I perceive my reality. All the seeds I have planted are being nurtured and are growing just as they should. And so it is. Amen.

47

Divine Guidance, thank you. I recognise the upgrades and as I witness the Divine Current flowing through the world, I know my part. And so I make this declaration to you. I demonstrate compassion, as everyone and everything is me. I choose love over fear, because I am of love, and it is my natural state of being. I acknowledge that the fear people feel is because of the way fear is being projected and although not in harmony with who we truly are, their fear is valid as it can be serving to reframe, plant seeds of desire, and bring awareness to where we have work to do. I choose to lead with empathy and remember my role as an all-encompassing being - to give more, to love more, and to lead more. I am grateful for this unravelling because it is our collective rebirth. I love you. Amen.

BLESSINGS ABOUND

48

Divine Guidance, I pray for you to lead the way to light. I thank you for your grace and your reminders that I am safe, supported, and held. I am asking for your hand, I acknowledge that your hand is always there, but right now I need to feel it more than ever. Show me the signs that you are with me. Let me see the path clearly. Let me lead with love. Let my fear dissipate as I remember that fear is an illusion and only love is real. Remind me that I am the rainbow after the storm, and that as the rainbow - I am beyond the storm, the product of the destruction. And in fact, destruction is highly creative - it is the catalyst for rebirth, for the memory of my Divinity. All as well. I remember who I am and I lead as love. And so it is. Amen.

49

Divine Guidance, I call upon your infinite love to engulf me. Let me feel love the way you feel love. Show me how to see everything as either an act of love or a call for love. Love is all, and love is the ultimate truth - teach me how to harness my Oneness, my Divinity, so that I can more fully step into my power. I honour this sacred experience in the three-dimensional, and I know that whatever limits the ego creates, my soul is always reminding me that I am limitless. I am infinite, that there are no bounds in an ever-expanding Universe, and that Universe is me. And so it is. Amen.

BLESSINGS ABOUND

50

*Divine Guidance, I thank you for this unravelling. Among all of the perceived fear, chaos, and destruction, you have allowed me to witness an immense sense of stillness, introspection, clarity, connection, Divinity, intuition, peace, and freedom. And I know that to realise these things, it means that I am vibrating at their frequencies. I acknowledge how far I've come and how powerful I really am. I remember that everything is Divinely Orchestrated and as long as I align with love, I am safe, held, and supported. The **blessings abound** and I am so grateful to feel blessed. Allow me to wake up blessed, go to sleep blessed, walk, talk, eat, move blessed. I love you. And so it is. Amen.*

BLESSINGS ABOUND

51

Divine Guidance, bring me back to love. Bring me back to my light. Allow courage, love, light, joy, and alignment to be my dominant thoughts and feelings. I welcome all that is for my highest good and the highest good of everyone involved into my life experience, with open arms. I am willing to feel my shadows if they are to be serving, but I will always remember who I am - and that is light. Transcending all experiences is my awareness of my higher self, of consciousness. This experience is unfolding just as it should, in Divine Order - my role is to maintain my alignment with that Divinity. And so it is. I love you. Amen.

BLESSINGS ABOUND

52

Divine Guidance, Blessings Abound. I am surrounded by beautiful, kind people and everything is working out best case scenario. I feel elated, I feel incredibly grateful. This life is so full, and I am savouring all of it. The food, the people, the books, the trees, the beach, the clothes, the make-up, the laughter, the music, the dancing. All of it. How fun it is. Thank you for allowing me this sacred experience. I honour it by realising just how profound it is. I love you. Amen.

53

Divine Guidance, I asked for clarity, so that I can clearly plant my seeds of desire daily and step-by-step, have my vibrational offering realise all that is in my physical reality. I know that everything that I want was planted there with the means to fulfil those desires. I am incredibly grateful for this journey and the people, places, and opportunities that present themselves along my journey to play their integral roles in this manifestation. I am in love with this life. And so it is. Amen.

54

Divine Guidance, today I make a declaration with you as my witness. I am on my Divine path - always supported and always guided. In moments of discomfort or doubt you offer me the people, opportunities, and inspired thoughts to help me pivot and reframe. I know that time is just a construct and I, as my Divine Self, work from beyond time, which means that it is always just the moment before the physical realisation. My main focus and priority is on maintaining my alignment, because I know that alignment precedes everything. I choose to step into my magnetic power everyday, and with your infinite Grace - I tune into my desired self, more and more each day. I am grateful. And so it is. Amen.

BLESSINGS ABOUND

55

Divine Guidance, I call upon your loving energy and Grace to be felt by me now. May I realise your hand in all that I do. May I have moments of Divine Realisation where I recognise my Spiritual Army supporting me, guiding me, loving me. Let the veil of illusion be lifted and may I see clearly with my third eye, as though I am looking through your eyes unto the world. And let all that I see feel the love that I am - and may that love be mirrored back to me. I call upon my eternal connection to the earth and her sacred spirits to hear my calls whenever I request their intervention. I declare that I will always remember that as I ask, my calling is received instantly - all that is then required is my alignment with its physical realisation. Thank you for this Divine Wisdom. I love you. And so it is. Amen.

BLESSINGS ABOUND

56

Divine Guidance, I call upon your light. Let me see it in myself - even when I think I can't. Let me feel alignment, as you know alignment, not as I have imagined it to be. Remind me, whenever the 3D world consumes me, that I am the stars, the sun, the moon, the sky. Remind me that I was born in perfect harmony, and any discord or resistance I feel is a byproduct of this world, and I have the means and power to move through the heaviness and feel my light once again. I call upon your light. Thank you. I love you. And so it is. Amen.

57

Divine Guidance, let us see through the eyes of love. Let us feel ourselves as we truly are. Let us be receptive to your messages. Let our intuitive nudges be so clear and so vivid that we would never be able to mistake them. Guide us on our path so that we shall never get it wrong. Bring to us what is rightfully ours, as we were already born into this world with them. Thank you for all that I am, all that I have, and all that I am becoming. I love you. And so it is. Amen.

58

Divine Guidance, allow the revelations to be for my highest good and for the highest good of everyone involved. Please allow me to hear, see, and feel the Divine messages that come from my higher self, so that I can fully trust and accept the intuitive nudges that come through and then act with conviction from those nudges. Please, whenever I waver, make it easy for me to come back to my Divinity. Today I choose to see and feel my own light, embodying the highest frequency of that which I am. I love you. And so it is. Amen.

BLESSINGS ABOUND

59

Divine Guidance, allow me to realise the light that exists within my vessel and let me remember that I was born healed, as I came into this world Divine and to tap into that Divinity, is merely to choose to. Allow me to see the ease in every decision, I trust my higher self to lead the way - my only job is to silence the internal chatter so that I can hear the intuitive nudges. There is nothing too big for me and everything that flows into my experience is Divinely Orchestrated, and simultaneously a reflection of my vibrational offering. I feel immense gratitude for your love and guidance. Thank you. I love you. And so it is. Amen.

60

Divine Guidance, everything I do leads to clarity, everything I say leads to alignment, everything I feel leads to a higher vibrational offering, and I know that all of that is because you work through me. My Divinity is certain, and the only thing I need to do in the present moment is feel the magnitude of gratitude for that which I am, for that which you are. And I am receiving all the time, just like the rivers are ever flowing, so are the energetic currents that are flowing to me, through me, for me, from me. There is one truth - and that truth is the part of me that I now intentionally allow in. Thank you. I love you. Amen.

BLESSINGS ABOUND

61

Divine Guidance, I call upon you to command the release of any resistance I may be holding on to. Allow me to shift more closer to my truest self, to release any attachment to lack or poverty, and realise my innate abundance and prosperity. I welcome my ever-flowing creative expression and the stream that follows that expression. I call upon you to shift my awareness from fear to faith - knowing that I am Divinely Guided and eternally led to the light. May all my intentions be of love and grow from love, to love, from love, through love. May I always find my way back home to you. I ask that you ease any resistance that exists within my vessel and give me the strength I need to move through it. I shower my body with love - and may you amplify that love to Godly proportions. And so it is. Amen.

62

Divine Guidance, I call upon you to witness my unbecoming. Unbecoming my conditions, limits, and seeming errors, and remembering my Divinity and the Source of that which I am, which is love. I ask for your hand moving forward, guide me to my path and let me feel the legions upon legions of support that comes from the spirit world. I am grateful for all the ways in which you show up for me now, I know everything is of you, but when I recognise the feathers, numbers, people, totems, I feel an immense sense of Divine Guidance. Thank you. I love you. Amen.

63

Divine Guidance, I call upon you to show me the path of light so that I can serve at my fullest capacity. Allow me to maintain a high vibrational offering, so that I can consciously and intentionally feel the Universe work through me. Help me remember that I am always a bright light shining and if ever I feel anything other than that, it is me just dimming my own light. Remind me that true gratitude is embodying the love that I am and sharing that love with the world. Thank you for guiding me to new heights and revealing the path that has always been within me. And so it is. Amen.

64

Divine Guidance, I pray that he/she feels the love that he/she is. I pray that any resistance to well-being dissipates. I pray that strength and enlightenment engulf him/her. I pray that he/she remembers the infinity of souls and that the temporary physical journey is designed to teach us love and when the soul is ready, we will always choose to move on. I pray that he/she is showered in Golden Light, so that his/her shadows see their own light. I pray that any perceived pain is healed. I pray that he/she remembers his/her own Divinity, and that remembering leads to joy, alignment, and unconditional love. May peace be upon him/her. And so it is. Amen.

*Channeled for when someone is about to transition
If you come across this prayer when you don't have someone on their transitioning journey, pray the prayer anyway, it will vibrationally be assigned to someone who needs it.

65

Divine Guidance, I pray that you lead the way. And as you offer no resistance, allow me to tap into that unrestricted supply. You have all the answers, allow the revelations to flow to me and through me easily and effortlessly. Let my vision for love expansion be the catalyst for every action that precedes that desire. Let everything I do have you in it; every seed I plant, every tree that bears fruit, every fruit that I eat and share with others. Let your love be felt in a way that I can understand it. Thank you. I love you. Amen.

BLESSINGS ABOUND

66

Divine Guidance, I pray that all is well. I pray that I have an innate knowing that everything is always well and that I remember that my perception will always be limited because of my human condition - but that I am simultaneously of you - therefore, the part of me that is Spirit, the part of me that offers no resistance, will always guide me. And my job is to surrender and listen to the intuitive guidance and maintain my alignment with it. I hear you. Thank you. I love you. And so it is. Amen.

67

Divine Guidance, I pray that you engulf us with your infinite love and allow us to be channels of your Divine Grace. Please allow the messages to be revealed in a way that we can understand and interpret them. We call for only love to exist within this sacred container, and for us to be protected. I call upon our angels, spirit guides, and ancestors to be present with love during this reading. And so it is. Amen.

68

My Soul Mate Devotional

I'm committed to you, our family, the life we are creating together, and our love. I commit to show up in this partnership - through the contrast and through the blessings. You inspire me to initiate and step into my highest state of alignment. And I pray that I mirror that for you too. You are my muse - and I commit to being yours too. I commit to always come from a place of love and compassion and seek to understand you on all levels. I will be patient and present with you - and commit to speaking a language we both understand. I commit to speaking my truth and my heart even when I perceive it to be hard. I allow myself to be vulnerable with you because I know I am safe with you - as you hold space for me in your empowered Divine Masculine energy - and allow me to be in my fluid Divine Feminine as a byproduct. I am committed to forever with you. I enter this with every intention to expand with you, grow with you, evolve with you, impact with

you, create with you, and celebrate with you. Our souls chose each other in this life - and in many before and many to come and I don't take that responsibility lightly. The codes, that we each carry which will be married and birthed in Union through our children, hold the keys to our lineage mastering their magic. Alone we are God in flesh, but together we are a potent elixir of magic and amplification which will forever change the Universe. I trust God's Will and trust that our paths are unfolding in Divine Light. I honour your role as the Divine Masculine; holding space, protecting, serving, creating safety and stability, grounding and rooting, letting me move through you. And I honour my role as the Divine Feminine; forever fluid and spontaneous, filling every crevice that you've created, amplifying everything that you already are, softening and melting into you, letting myself be fully seen by you. May we forever illuminate each other - revealing what is hidden, nurturing this connection. I commit to letting you lead with love and I trust the path that we move on together. I commit to our intimate desire for each other, fully expressed through a passionate dance together. When we come together, we will always be more. It is safe to love you and to be loved by you. I am devoted to our love.

BLESSINGS ABOUND

69

Divine Guidance, I call upon you to guide me into the shadows safely with the loving support of my Spiritual Team. May I only be offered what I have the capacity to receive – and may you determine that capacity. Whenever I feel myself get lost in my own shadow or confronted by it, wanting to reject it, remind me to centre back into love. Love as you love. From this place, all paths are illuminated, and I maintain a sense of neutrality – allowing all experiences at will to pass through my experience, lovingly directing them as I feel called. And may that calling always be your hand navigating the path through me. I release any resistance and rejection I have held to experiencing the depths of my self, because I recognise that you exist within everything - even in the shadows. Thank you. I love you. And so it is. Amen.

BLESSINGS ABOUND

70

Divine Guidance, remind me that your way isn't always the way I choose or the way I feel is best, and yet your way is the way. So I ask that you make the path crystal clear – so I'm never to miss it. I want what is for my highest good, and I trust that what's for me will always be mine. And if it's not for me, don't have me want it. I trust that your perspective will always be more clear than mine, so I commit to connecting with you daily so that you can show me the way. And even as I explore the shadowy depths, I trust that you have led me there, in Divine Order, protected by Divine Providence. Even in the darkest darkness, I am safe, because I know you are with me. I open myself up to explore all parts of myself, and as I do this, make it as light and fun as possible. As I know you will if I allow it. I love you. Thank you. And so it is. Amen.

BLESSINGS ABOUND

71

Divine Guidance, forever remind me that time is not linear, and if once activated, a code is eternally accessible by me. I consciously choose to access and activate all codes that are serving now. And as I continue to evolve and expand, remind me that this moment is exactly as it should be, nothing more, grander, or more profound is required. Remind me that the illusion of reality is the one I have created in my Mind's Eye – and I have the power to shift my perceived reality at will. Thank you for connecting me with Soul Family in this incarnation - we have not overlooked our Divine Mission, in fact we devote our life to honouring this mission. Make it easy for us to tap into your supply, and make it even easier for us to know exactly who to share it with. I ask that my awareness of what's possible drift beyond my conscious mind's horizon, I ask that you reveal to me parts of you that I have yet to access. I am ready now. Thank you. I love you. And so it is. Amen.

BLESSINGS ABOUND

72

Divine Guidance, as I move through the intricate threads of my destiny, I recognise you in everything. I see that all of this was for me exclusively. It's all designed in my favour – all I need to do is to make love to it all. To see you in everything, is to see me in everything, and to see you, is to recognise that even at the deepest depth, and the darkest dark, you are there, offering me more of me to understand. The grand design is grander than I could ever understand, but I don't need to. Instead, I allow myself to unfold within every experience, letting it teach me how to recognise you, because it was made just for me. I allow myself to see how it's all in my favour. Under the gaze of your loving Grace - I accept all of it. My perceptions teach me my capacity to experience humanness. It is my greatest honour and joy to feel all of it. Thank you for reminding me that it is all serving and all for my highest good. Oh the fun that is to be had. Thank you. I love you. And so it is. Amen.

BLESSINGS ABOUND

73

Divine Guidance, I feel hugged by you, safe in your loving arms as I continue to bridge the gap between my mortal self and my immortal self. Knowing that both exist simultaneously, and both offer me exactly what is required on this journey. I relinquish any and all doubt, fear and resistance that may have held a barrier between me and what is mine. As I consciously step into the light now, honouring the shadows that come with me, I accept you fully. And on my path of light, I am awakened to infinity – previously to truly understanding the volume of infinity, and still being limited by my human filter, and yet the best understanding I've ever had. And within that pool of infinity, that I too exist within, everything is within arms reach, and as you've offered me time and time again, I need only choose it and it's mine. Not just what I perceive as physical, but anything that is energy, which is everything. The feeling, the personality, the people, the feature, all of it. And as I choose, I call you to choose through me, aligning me with the highest outcome. Thank you. I love you. And so it is. Amen.

BLESSINGS ABOUND

74

Divine Guidance, I call upon my next cycle, I welcome it lovingly and I am ready to release anything standing in the way of my highest timeline. I feel the shift, and may you amplify it. I feel deeply called to open myself up to you completely, and I trust the pathway you have laid out for me. I see the messages you offer me - through people, places, songs, nature, numbers, and animals, and each one offers me something profound. Through you, I ask that my Spiritual Team communicate with me loudly, and any veil between me and my Team of Light, and light only, is lifted. May I feel safe in their presence, knowing that they exist as expressions of you, devoted to the light. May I lean into your simplicity, I know the human experience distorts and creates complexities, but you offer me your love in the most simplest ways and may I mirror that offering to the world. May I eternally be a pillar of your light, devoted to the light, and always patiently eager for the expansion of you, as a Divine expression of you. Hear this as my call for my next unfolding. Thank you. I love you. And so it is. Amen.

BLESSINGS ABOUND

75

Divine Guidance, reveal to me the truth I've always known, that it gets to be easy, that it gets to be effortless, but not without effort. I call upon you to enhance my power to cultivate and realise my desires, as though the infinite choices are mine for the taking. And as I select the desired pathway, align my desire with my highest timeline. I feel magnetic, I feel powerful, I feel your infinity pulsing through my veins – now show me how to use it. Show me the short cuts, and I will show the whole world. Show me how powerful I am. Work through me to reveal life's miracles and blessings. I know I embody this, if ever I start to lose sight of my power, offer me a subtle yet undeniable sign that it is all available for me. May everything I say and do be amplified because it has your light within it. I am you embodied – may I always act accordingly. I love you. Thank you. And so it is. Amen.

BLESSINGS ABOUND

76

Divine Guidance, move through me. Reveal to me your sacred light. May Elohim be my daily prayer to invoke your light within me. And as I radiate that light I call upon all that is to be known by me. May I open myself up to the wisdom I contain within, for even the smallest photons carry codes, and may I also open myself up to the wisdom I can access without, for even the farthest reaching stars carry codes designed for me alone. May this sacred ritual move me to the spaces designed for my highest experience, may I see the light within all expressions of you, and may any perceived darkness transmute itself before my eyes, and I as its witness, vow to use its new found light to bestow glory and light upon the world. For no expression of you is too small to be witnessed and shared. This I pledge to you as I honour these elements that you have offered as extensions of you, just so that I can know you. Thank you, I love you, And so it is, Amen.

BLESSINGS ABOUND

77

Divine Guidance, to pray a prayer asking for what's unknown seems like an impossible feat. How am I to know the words to use when they don't exist yet? And yet I know with certainty that you will offer them to me, because I am never denied even the farthest request. It is all accessible to me, and it's right now that I realise that, that includes everything that hasn't been accessible by anyone yet. How am I to know what hasn't been thought by anyone ever before? You will guide me in that knowing. It won't just feel foreign to me, but I will ponder the words to use to describe the revelations. And you will simultaneously reveal to me how known these truths are to my infinite self. I am open to the unravelling of this sacred journey, I surrender control and I allow myself to flow with your direction. I vow to be an open channel, and may I confront all rejection of truth by redirecting my focus back upon you. Forever your conduit. Thank you. I love you. And so it is. Amen

BLESSINGS ABOUND

78

Divine Guidance, may I feel the Divine veil protecting me, cloaking me with your light. I recognise that my relationship with you isn't designed to be understood by anyone else - it is an intimacy that only I can know. There are some things that only God and I are to experience together. This entire cosmic web is designed for me alone to understand. And I trust you. I trust that you will eternally imprint me with the knowing required to navigate my unfolding here on earth. My human self may not always perceive it as easy - and yet it is. You will grace me with reminders of your effortless ease and flow. May I remind myself that the cosmic dance isn't to be predictable, but instead spontaneously enjoyed. May I look at the beauty I find on this planet and see you within it, reminding me that your magic is always at my fingertips. May I make every moment, every thing, and every one Holy. Your grandness and perfect orchestration can be found in even the smallest flower petals. And may I bask in the glory of this world's beauty. I am as I am, and I am you. Thank you. I love you. And so it is. Amen.

BLESSINGS ABOUND

79

Divine Guidance, I call upon you to remind us of our Divine Unity, we flow as one body, never separate from the cosmic current, and as I intentionally choose to tap into that Divinely flowing current, everything that you plant in my mind as a perceived desire is realised in this time space reality. I ask that this experience is filled with the juices of life; fun, spontaneity, love, exploration, connection. And while we remember our connection to the infinite supply, let us feel your infinite love. Let us feel love the way you feel love. Show us how to see everything as either an act of love or a call for love. Love is all, and love is the ultimate truth, we come from love and to love we shall return, and our journey here is an expression of that love, an expansion of that love - teach us how to harness our Oneness, our Divinity, so that we can more fully step into our power. We honour this sacred experience in the 3 Dimensional, and we know that whatever limits the ego creates, our soul is always reminding us that we are limitless, we are infinite, that there are no bounds in an ever expanding Universe, and that Universe is me, is you, is all of us. We are but one body. And so it is. I love you. Amen.

BLESSINGS ABOUND

80

Divine Guidance, I release the burdens that I have placed upon others. May any expectations I have held on another dissipate and cease to exist. May I see everyone as I see you - an infinite boundless love, and may my love for you, and your love for me, be how I offer love to others, with that same depth and intensity. May I see the world as my mirror, either as a mirror of my own projections, or as a mirror of my perceptions, either way offering me an illumination. It's all serving me as I have chosen how to interact with this world, and it offers me what I need in every moment. As my true nature will always be supported in this world. Nothing nor no one can deny me access to you. I need only release anything I have accumulated as untrue, and all that will be left is you. May my relationships with others be as my relationship with you is - and may I remember that there are no others. I am intimately dancing with self, playfully interacting with my many faces, and so to condemn any of me, is to condemn all of me, and so I practice acceptance and love - as it is, is as it should be. I love you. Thank you. And so it is. Amen.

BLESSINGS ABOUND

81

Divine Guidance, release anything that I'm holding onto that isn't mine. Release anything that has been trapped in my body as density. I call in the light and watch the density dissolve itself and wash out from my body. I welcome your Divine Light and feel your light begin to multiply within me. I accept myself as I am and surrender completely to your will. And my will is your will. And I will for light to enfold me. I feel myself become engulfed by light. I feel myself become lighter and lighter. And as you wash over me and within me, your light becomes me - I feel it as truth. And the heaviness I once carried now leaves only space for light to fill it. I offer love to the heaviness I have released, as I watch it now transmute into light, now offering itself as a powerful source of light which can now be weaved into the cosmic fabric as it had always been designed to be weaved. I am grateful to witness the metamorphosis of what I had perceived to be density. May the light always be known by me and may any perception of density, darkness, or shadow offer me a deeper, richer understanding of you. I need not be afraid. As it is all you. I love you. Thank you. And so it is. Amen.

BLESSINGS ABOUND

82

Divine Guidance, as I walk through the portal of light, reveal to me all truths that are to be known by me right now. All truths are truth. But I ask to see as you see. Offer me a wider, higher perspective of truth. Reveal to me the truth of the higher densities so that I can observe as you observe. Not so that I can contain more, but so that I can understand myself more. The wider the perspective of truth, the more I can understand how limited our idea of truth is. Allowing me to surrender to your guidance for only you can know the ultimate truth. And to see any truth as a different truth is to perceive separation. As all truths are infinite fragments of your one all-encompassing truth, one I need not ever know in its entirety, because it offers itself to me in fragments that I can comprehend and hold space for. And I also ask that you use me. Use me as your Divine vessel to project your light upon the world. And in return, the light that you project through me, is the light that I am and that I maintain within myself, drawing unto it everything that matches that light. I love you. Thank you. And so it is. Amen.

83

Divine Guidance, I call upon you to guide me in surrendering control. Remind me that life alone is the miracle. That every breath holds with it the infinite wisdom of the Divine and all that is required of me to tap into that infinity is to witness the now, and as I do, you open up worlds for me, giving me access to all that is and all that will be, because it has always been. It's easy when I let it be easy. And as I perceive a human timeline, remind me that there is just one universal timeline that transcends all time and space. There is no hurry in infinity, and so I need not create the illusion of limitations. I am of the boundless. It's all in perfect order, right on time, right on track. Can I revel in the unfolding without needing it to be different? May the reminders to surrender be soft and yet direct. I trust you. Thank you. I love you. And so it is. Amen.

BLESSINGS ABOUND

84

Divine Guidance, experiencing the richness of this beautiful 3D yet Godly world is to experience your depths of wisdom. It is to know you through this world. Nothing here is conventionally 3D and yet it all is. Because they allow me to integrate your Divine Wisdom through them, allowing me to more easily experience my humanness. May I always welcome my human experience with open arms and an open heart, reminding myself just how much light wanted to collapse itself into matter to know itself as a different expression of self. And I have been blessed to be on the forefront of this desire to know myself in this way. And may I never take it for granted as it gifts me the pleasures of the 3D world. The flowers, bees, birds, and dragonflies wanted to know me, interact with me, and so I am here; to play, to dance, to sing, to frolic, to love. What a way to learn to know myself. Thank you. I love you. And so it is. Amen.

BLESSINGS ABOUND

85

Divine Guidance, I pray for Safe Expansion. A safe determined by you. May it be beyond my capacity to imagine and simultaneously may it be an expansion that my etheric body has energetically prepared for. Living in the beautiful harmony of unknown and unpredictable, and expected and familiar. I allow myself to be a conduit for your light and also a vessel for your natural design for expansion. May this moment be the genesis of a light unexpected in the most light-filled way, may it be beyond any horizons I had imagined and may I now eternally know the power I have access to when I will it into existence. Show me how powerful I am. Show me what's possible when I believe. Show me how easy it can be. And I vow to share that light with others, because I recognise that there are no others, and as I expand, we all expand. May I recognise that expansion isn't just outwardly growing but also inwardly - may I forever go deeper and deeper into myself; which is the Universe incarnate, to know the richness and depth I am a part of. I accept my role as God in Flesh - a fragment of you. And so it is. Thank you. I love you. Amen.

BLESSINGS ABOUND

86

Divine Guidance, as I hold space for you, I hold space for love. I call upon you to amplify the love that exists within all my connections; past, present, and future, the eternal now. I trust that you offer me protection and deflect anything that is not of love. May all Divine Unions that I enter be protected by your Divine Light. May my connections feel harmonious and balanced, honouring the Divine Feminine and Divine Masculine polarity that exists within all of us. May all my earthly connections remind me that they exist in the ethereal just as much as they exist in the physical - and that my perception of a connection is just one perceived expression of the connection - and that in fact what God sees is far beyond my capacity to witness. And so I trust in your direction. I am certain that you are always guiding me towards the most profound love and relationships - so that I can know you in a way that I have never before. My heart is open and welcomes your love. Love is safe. I love you. Thank you. And so it is. Amen.

BLESSINGS ABOUND

87

Divine Guidance, I call upon you to amplify the peace and harmony I feel within me. As I focus on my breath and my inner stillness, I witness the peace and stillness of all things as mirrors of my Divine Self. I recognise that God is Me. I feel the infinity of God's love flowing through me. I am allowing more of myself to be realised. Show me the way to my Higher Self. If it is of love, reveal it to me. I am so grateful to experience and align with the frequency of all my desires, recognising that they have been planted intentionally by God. I allow it to be easy. I call upon you to remind me that I am always in alignment. When I offer moments of resistance let me see them as blessings that lead to me focus. As I pray upon this intention, I feel aligned with love, well-being, peace, harmony, and abundance. Thank you. I love you. And so it is. Amen.

BLESSINGS ABOUND

88

Divine Guidance, I am witnessing the flood of blessings wash over me. I feel the infinite and absolute love flow to and through me. I am always protected by this Divine Love. I pray that you infuse me with your Golden Light, and as it enters my body, it amplifies the light I already am, offering me the ability to self-heal and align with the highest version of myself. I also call upon you to create a shield around my vessel, protecting me, allowing only the frequencies of Divine Light and Love to enter my field. I call upon you to remind me of my innate abundance, remind me to witness the abundance that surrounds me, and to remember that I am of that same Source. I welcome the natural flow of abundance into my experience and I see it as here for me now and forever. May I eternally witness the light codes within all things and may you offer their healing light to me when I am in need. I walk this journey alongside you. Thank you. I love you. And so it is. Amen.

BLESSINGS ABOUND

89

Divine Guidance, I give myself to you and I trust that you will lead me to where is most serving. I need not be afraid of the natural unfolding because your hand is grander than my perception and I am certain that the Divine Web is designed in my favour. Have me release anything that is keeping me from your Divine Light. I allow myself to feel your Divine Light moving through my body as if my cells have become pure light form. My perceived confusion at times is a symptom of your Divine Revelation, teaching me to be patient and trusting. I am curious and open to the ways in which you wish to work through me, as your wish for me is my wish for myself. As I continue to clear space and release what is no longer serving, I feel your light brighten within me and I can use that light to be of service in the most powerful way. Show me how bright my light shines, have it be easy for me to witness my own light and to see that light reflected back to me through others. Thank you. I love you. And so it is. Amen.

90

Divine Guidance, let me be as you are. When I find myself lost in this world, may you remove the illusion of confusion from my mind. Have me see it as you see it - crystal clear. Illuminate the pathway so brightly that it would be impossible to miss it. Nudge me in the trajectory of that pathway in a gentle yet powerful way. May my thoughts be your thoughts - have me think from your perspective of understanding. Remove the obstacles, illusions, and falsehoods that blind my path, whisper your sweet whispers to me and offer me signs so I know that I'm naturally flowing, and have me perceive it as easy and organic. It gets to be easy. Show me how easy it is. Thank you. I love you. And so it is. Amen.

BLESSINGS ABOUND

91

Divine Guidance, as I dive into my own depths, hold me. As I soften my resistance to my own shadows, have me play intimately with them. As I explore the hidden parts of myself, offer your light. As I allow myself to be seen, open my heart to compassion. You have known me longer than I have known myself, and so I trust that you will show me the highest path. I recognise that my reflection will always be distorted and scaled, because how am I to truly see all that I am, in my grandness. And yet I trust that I will be shown enough in this moment, as though it were the perfect medicine for the now. I will not keep myself from accepting your guidance and light. I let myself open and unfold; how am I to fear anything that is of you. I am free to explore myself and I am safe in your loving presence. And so it is. I love you. Amen.

BLESSINGS ABOUND

92

Divine Guidance, I call upon your light for immediate protection and healing. I call upon the love and energy of all my ancestors in all my timelines. I call for the Universe to protect me, for Earth to protect me, for my Higher Self to protect me. I am Divinely protected. I declare that right now I release any and all energies, thoughts, and intentions that no longer service the highest good - be them mine or another. I cleanse myself and this space of negativity or anything not of love across all planes of existence, universes, and lifetimes. I call back my power from any contracts that have been made that are not of service or light. Let your Divine Light and protection bathe me. In gratitude, love, wellness, and peace. Only love may exist here. And so it is. I love you. Thank you. Amen.

93

Divine Guidance, I am being gifted more than I could ever truly acknowledge. More light, more codes, more revelations, more soul, more access. In this receptive state I create space by releasing anything that has been that is no longer required. I prepare for the beauty and blessings each new day offers by holding you front of mind. With you as my guide, I am led. With you as my guide, I am healed, because you offered me the gift of self-healing. I trust that the contract I desired for this life is being fulfilled and you offer me the pathways to fulfil it. I open myself up to you, lovingly surrendering as I await your messages. And in this place I witness your messages all around me; not just as wisdom, but as people, places, events, sounds, smells, and tastes. You are everywhere and I am never without. Remind me to play in my humanness because that is your greatest gift of all. I am here and now. And so it is. I love you. Thank you. Amen.

BLESSINGS ABOUND

94

Divine Guidance, where I perceive empty space, fill it with your love. Remind me to recognise that if it is all me, then I can never be truly lost or missing. I am whole, even in my confusion. And as you continue to show me the pieces of myself that I perceive as outside of me - show me that they have always been here and available to me. To witness your natural abundant supply, I must acknowledge my relationship with you, Source. And my relationship with you offers me a relationship with all other extensions of you. I am patient and compassionate with myself as I move through this journey of reclamation. There is no hurry in infinity, and to find myself, I need only look for you within everything, because you are home. As I continue to integrate and evolve, soften my perceived pain and perception of lack, show me how abundant I truly am. Thank you. I love you. And so it is. Amen.

BLESSINGS ABOUND

95

Divine Guidance, to forgive as God forgives, is to know that no wrong has been done. I am inherently flawed in my nature - not because I as human am flawed, but because my perceptions are flawed due to the distortions I carry. In our true essence, it is all perfectly orchestrated, and I can never change what has happened, but I can change the way I perceive what has happened. I forgive all of me, because I did what I could with what I had. And I forgive all of everyone, because their true nature is love, and no part of love is imperfect. I get to decide how I feel, I am empowered. I will not concede to the idea that someone can make me feel a certain way. And yet in my flawed perceptions, sometimes I feel hurt - remind me in that time of perceived pain, that I am in fact in control - and I can will my way into a different perception. You are full of Grace, and as I am you, so am I. Thank you. I love you. And so it is. Amen.

BLESSINGS ABOUND

96

Divine Guidance, open me up, so that the natural flow of creation pours through me. I am intrinsically creative, as my design is expansion, and in this 3D world I expand by creating. Allow me to tap into the infinite portals of creativity, where there are no limits and only boundless worlds where fantasy becomes reality through thought and intent. May my creative nature heal, may it flow effortlessly from my body, may it embody my soul's passionate nature to be more of itself. May you remind me that this world truly is the holographic reality that I have decided to create. I am an artist, I am the creator, the created, and the observer. I get to interact with life from all perspectives. There is so much beauty to be found in all my creations, and as they pour through me, I am offering the world magical codes that allow others to tap into that beauty alongside me. May I eternally enjoy the creation process, and may I see all moments as opportunities to create. To create is to birth love into this world, to make thought tangible. May all things be art to me and may my art lead the way. Thank you. I love you. And so it is. Amen.

BLESSINGS ABOUND

97

Divine Guidance, make it easy for me to move through density. I accept its purpose, its Divine teachings, and my need to move through it. But reveal to me the spaces in which releasing it is easy. I am healed because I am the healer. You have offered me the power to transmute all energy at will; be that physical, emotional or spiritual. I release what isn't mine to carry anymore, be that mine or another. May that release be transmuted into love and may I witness that love offer itself back into the collective that I'm a part of. May what was once perceived pain and buried density, now be love and light codes that I open myself up to receiving. May I remind myself that I heal from a place of wholeness - it's not what is broken, but what is preventing me from experiencing my wholeness. May I be gently reminded that all my emotions are held, loved, stored, and observed in every single cell in my body. My cells contain an emotional memory. So as I shift my relationship with my moving spectrum of emotions, the way in which they are stored and observed also shifts into a more balanced and integrated state. I am aware of self and my perceptions. I trust my changing perceptions. I don't hold onto old beliefs

BLESSINGS ABOUND

and identities. I allow myself to be shown another way. Thank you. I love you. And so it is. Amen.

BLESSINGS ABOUND

98

Divine Guidance, I call upon my ancestors of light. I want to honour all the ways in which they paved the way for me, planted seeds for me, healed for me, prayed for me. My blood is their blood, and so they live through me. I call upon my ancestors in all timelines, in all realities, even those beyond the human experience. May my devotion to expansion show them that everything is more because of them. I thank them for the Divine Wisdom they freely offer me, the protection and shielding from anything not of service, and for the work they do on my behalf in the Spiritual World. They have protected and redirected me in ways that I could never imagine. I am the descendant of the people who knew you intimately - who knew you in a way that we have now forgotten, but I vow to remember as it lives in my genetic memory, and through that memory I reconnect with the land spirits, the Elements, the animals, the ethers, and you. I am their prayer made manifest - and now I become the ancestor offering this sacred bloodline offering of light to my descendants. I'm honoured to have them live through me. Thank you. I love you. And so it is. Amen.

BLESSINGS ABOUND

99

Divine Guidance, I am free. I declare myself free and sovereign. I claim and reclaim all parts of me, wherever they currently reside. I free my body and my mind from enslavement. I am protected as I free myself. I am not attached to anything, I am of the eternal and nothing within the eternal can be held hostage without consent. And I do not give consent for bondage. I am connected to the infinite and eternal reality, where I am free and whole. My declared freedom is the freedom for all; past, present, future. And it's through my own emancipation that I free the world from their own confinements. Remind me that it is the mind that they wish to claim, but you nor I allow it. I have been assigned this path, so that I can show people true liberation. May any violations that deny my sovereignty be cleansed and restored into light and space. May those who wish to deny or reject my claim of freedom, receive your loving gentle whisper of wisdom, redirecting their thoughts into a loving openness, softening their heart, so that they too begin to feel free. As you are free, so am I. Thank you. I love you. And so it is. Amen.

BLESSINGS ABOUND

100

Divine Guidance, as I move throughout this world, protect me, in the physical, the astral, and all other energetic bodies. Shield me with white and Golden Light. Engulf me with your light. May every space that I'm led to, be directed by you. May I remember that you are omnipresent and so you are already wherever I am going. Bless my journey with the right places, people, and experiences, that align me with my highest evolution. Remind me to be patient and kind on my journey, as compassion welcomes in love. My mind has been blessed with an imagination that can dream up any space, and my body allows me to travel there with ease, and so I know that the journey is Divinely Orchestrated. I call upon my team of angels for protection and guidance, make their presence known to me today. Wherever I go - my shield of light goes with me, and it is already where I am to be, and it also remains where I leave. I trust that all the right people will be supporting me on my journeys and that my angels will nudge me when a redirection is required. Any delays are your Divine Intervention - and I trust you. Thank you. I love you. And so it is. Amen.

BLESSINGS ABOUND

VOLUME TWO

BLESSINGS ABOUND

This book has been created over many years, many channels, many deep intimate moments with God. The words are codes, they are medicine, they are light form embodied into expressed art. And they are for you. And so I invite you now to join me in submitting one of your own channelled prayers, where I will collate all the submissions to create Volume Two (and all subsequent volumes) of Blessings Abound.

Before submitting, please make sure they are your words, that you have the right to use them and share them. By submitting you also agree for us to use your words in our next publication, you will be quoted, but you will hold no rights to the book, but you will be able to use your own prayer in whichever ways you desire.

To make a submission, visit:

grigoriakritsotelis.com/prayers

BLESSINGS ABOUND

1

To show you the kind of submissions we will be accepting, here is our first submission for Volume Two, channelled by my dear friend Tenealle Alexander (IG @teneallealexander_)

Divine guidance, We pray that you will shine your light of love, protection, and prosperity over our household. May this house at the address of _____ be covered in your light, protected from all entities of dark nature. As your light shines down on us, may it transmute any darkness back to light as it originally was. Enhancing the blessings that are available to us in each passing moment. To have us all anchored in love and safety so that we may heal our nervous systems and gain the courage to pursue our deepest dreams and desires. May only the purest of beings who intend to support us on our journeys and serve us and our highest good be welcome in this home. May this home be a place of holiness mirroring back your divinity onto us as we are made of Source and are one with you at our deepest core always. We thank you deeply for your love, for the small reminders that you are always with us. For the ability to forever grow deeper connected to you and your divinity and trust that you

BLESSINGS ABOUND

will continue to guide us towards our highest selves. And so it is. Amen.

BLESSINGS ABOUND

FINAL WORDS

Prayer is powerful because it summons energy into a focused intention. It calls upon angels, ancestors of light, your Galactic family, your Spirit Team, your Spirit Guides, Ascended Masters, God, light, and love. It is magic, alchemy, a dance with the Divine. It offers you God's Eye View, it activates the God Switch.

Each prayer was prayed for someone or many, each prayer was graciously offered by God and my Spirit Team, each prayer asked of me, for it to be shared with you. And each prayer asks of you, to birth your own channelled prayer.

Each prayer has been activated, and each prayer offers medicine and healing codes. These aren't just words on a page, they are hours and hours of intimate moments with God. They have offered themselves to you. And they will continue to, across many lifetimes.

As you pray these prayers, you pray for everyone, past, present, and future. As you pray these prayers, you offer the collective your light.

May you remember your light, as you're in pure receivership of this Divine Wisdom.

ABOUT THE AUTHOR

GRIGORIA KRITSOTELIS

Grigoria Kritsotelis, Spiritual Teacher. She is dedicated to raising the vibration of the earth by spreading the message of light and love.

Grigoria has mastered her craft in the Spiritual arena and applies spiritual practices to all her teachings. She is a thought leader, creative intellect, and has a magnetic light-filled energy that demands the attention from any room she enters. She has used these skills to speak on stages, host retreats and events, and create hundreds of training content to serve her audience. Her focus is on creating a sacred safe space for people to reconnect with their true selves, remove their limiting beliefs that come from misguided thoughts and teachings, and return to a state of alignment with the vibrational frequency of love.

Grigoria isn't just a teacher of spirituality, she embodies the light-filled energy she teaches and commits to sharing her knowledge on reprogramming the subconscious mind, and living a Spiritually-led life, so that everyone can consciously live a life they desire.

A message from Gee

My goal in life is to be one of those people who are just light. You see them and you suddenly feel so warm inside, and all you want to do is hug them. And they look at you and smile with the warmest light in their eyes... and you love them. Not in a romantic way, but you just want to be close to them and you hope some of their light transfers onto you.

www.grigoriakritsotelis.com

Other books by Grigoria:

God is Me: The path to enlightenment through self-reflection

God is Me has been written as a collection of notes and reflections, so unlike a traditional book structure, there is no beginning, middle or end.

6.02 billion people all over the world believe in God in some form. Probably more if you were to refer to God as a synonym for Universe, angels, source, infinite intelligence, energy, cosmos or whatever truth aligns with you, which is what I do in God is Me. God is Me, is a reflective piece of writing based on the concept of enlightenment through self-reflection. The realisation that in fact I may not be God, but God is me. And once I become self-aware, that is, aware that I possess the same unlimited power that God does, and that power lives within me, within all of us, and the only thing that I need to do to access that power is to align with my own well-being, my own joy, I am finally free. Free to live intentionally instead of by default.

God is Me isn't to evoke a learning experience as much as it is to allow for the reader to remember what they already know within the depths of their soul. A book about our re-connection to the One Source.

www.ingramcontent.com/pod-product-compliance
Lightning Source LLC
Chambersburg PA
CBHW062046290426
44109CB00027B/2749